NOTE TO PARENTS

Welcome to Kingfisher Readers! This program is designed to help young readers build skills, confidence, and a love of reading as they explore their favorite topics.

These tips can help you get more from the experience of reading books together. But remember, the most important thing is to make reading fun!

Tips to Warm Up Before Reading

- Ask your child to share what they already know about the topic.
- Preview the pages, pictures, sub-heads, and captions, so your reader will have an idea what is coming.
- Share your questions. What are you both wondering about?

While Reading

- Stop and think at the end of each section. What was that about?
- Let the words make pictures in your minds. Share what you see.
- When you see a new word, talk it over. What does it mean?
- Do you have more questions? Wonder out loud!

After Reading

- Share the parts that were most interesting or surprising.
- Make connections to other books, similar topics, or experiences.
- Discuss what you'd like to know more about. Then find out!

With five distinct levels and a wealth of appealing topics, the Kingfisher Readers series provides children with an exciting way to learn to read about the world around them. Enjoy!

Ellie Costa, M.S. Ed.
Literacy Specialist, Bank Street School for Children, New York

KINGFISHER
READERS

level
5

The Changing Environment

Deborah Chancellor

KINGFISHER
NEW YORK

KINGFISHER
LONDON & NEW YORK

Copyright © Kingfisher 2014
Published in the United States by Kingfisher,
175 Fifth Ave., New York, NY 10010
Kingfisher is an imprint of Macmillan Children's Books, London.
All rights reserved.

Distributed in the U.S. and Canada by Macmillan,
175 Fifth Ave., New York, NY 10010

Library of Congress Cataloging-in-Publication data
has been applied for.

Series editor: Thea Feldman
Literacy consultant: Ellie Costa, Bank Street School for Children, New York

ISBN: 978-0-7534-7152-4 (HB)
ISBN: 978-0-7534-7153-1 (PB)

Kingfisher books are available for special promotions
and premiums. For details contact: Special Markets
Department, Macmillan, 175 Fifth Ave., New York, NY 10010.

For more information, please visit www.kingfisherbooks.com

Printed in China
9 8 7 6 5 4 3 2 1
1TR/0314/WKT/UG/105MA

Picture credits

The Publisher would like to thank the following for permission to reproduce their material. Every care has been taken to trace copyright holders. However, if there have been unintentional omissions or failure to trace copyright holders, we apologize and will, if informed, endeavor to make corrections in any future edition.
Top = t; Bottom = b; Center = c; Left = l; Right = r
Cover Corbis/Reuters; cover t KF Archive; Cover c Shutterstock (SS)/Juriah Mosin; Cover b Corbis/Radius; 2l Corbis/Reuters; 2lc Corbis/Ocean; 2c Corbis/Joel Sartore/NGS; 2cr Corbis/Radius; 2r Alamy/Gary Crabbe; 3l Corbis/Radius; 3cl Alamy/Ariadne Van Zandbergen; 3c SS/Matt Jones; 3cr KF Archive (KF); 3r Photoshot/Xinhua News Agency; 4l SS/beata becia; 4–5 KF; 6 SS/Anton Foltin; 7 KF; 8 SS/Juriah Mosin; 9 Corbis/Radius; 10 SS/Antonio S.; 11 Corbis/Ocean; 12 KF; 13t Corbis/DLILL; 13b Corbis/Radius; 14 SS/Loskutnikov; 15 SS/fotohunter; 16 Corbis/Ocean; 17tl KF; 17b SS/achios; 18cl Corbis/Peter Andrews/Reuters; 18bl SS Fedor Korolevsky; 18br SS Danii Balashov; 19 KF; 20 SS/Ian Bracegirdle; 21 SS/Dmitry Berkut or /pzRomashka; 22tl Photoshot/NHPA; 22b SS/Rafael Ramiraz Lee; 23 Corbis/STR/Reuters; 24 Getty/BAL; 25t Corbis/DLILL; 25b Getty/Science Faction Jewels; 26 Alamy/Steve Morgan; 27t Corbis/Julie Dermansky; 27b Corbis/Joel Sartore/NGS; 28 Corbis/Reuters; 29t Getty/Flickr; 29b Corbis/David Frazier; 30 Photoshot/Xinhua News Agency; 31 SS/Volodynyr Golnyk; 33t SS/Caitlin Mirra; 33b Alamy/Ariadne Van Zandbergen; 34tr Corbis/Pete Oxford; 35 Alamy/Gary Crabbe; 36 KF; 37 SS/Eric Gevaert; 38 Shutterstock/Otmar Smit; 39t Photoshot; 39b KF; 40 SS/Matt Jones; 41 SS/Dmitry Naumov; 42 Alamy/Jenny Matthews; 43 Corbis/Surf; 44 Getty/Lifesize; 45t Getty/First Life; 45b SS/Valery Kraynov; 45b SS/Quang Ho; 45b SS/TigerForce; 45b SS/Denis Larkin; 46l Corbis/Reuters; 46lc Corbis/Ocean; 46c Corbis/Joel Sartore/NGS; 46cr Corbis/Radius; 46r Alamy/Gary Crabbe; 47l Corbis/Radius; 47cl Alamy/Ariadne Van Zandbergen; 47c SS/Matt Jones; 47cr KF; 47r Photoshot/Xinhua News Agency.

Contents

Wonderful world

We use the word "environment" in many different ways. When we talk about the environment, we often just mean our immediate surroundings—everything around us that we can see, smell, taste, touch, and hear.

Howler monkey

Blue morpho butterfly

The environment is all around us.

However, the word "environment" can mean something much bigger than that. It can mean all of the things that we need in order to stay alive. This means the land that we live on, the air that we breathe, the food that we eat, and the water that we drink. It can even mean the entire natural world.

Fig tree

All of the living things on Earth, as well as the places where they live, make up the environment. Life is found all over the world, in the hottest, coldest, driest, and wettest places. In order to survive, animals and plants must be able to **adapt** to the places where they live. This is easier in some parts of the world than it is in others.

Amazon rainforest

Rainforests are **tropical** forests with heavy rainfall. A rainforest environment is warm and wet and provides perfect living conditions for many things.

Coati

Poison-arrow frog

Basilisk lizard

5

Life on Earth

There is an amazing variety of life on Earth. This variety is called biodiversity, and it is an important feature of the natural environment. Some places have more **species** (types) of animals, plants, **bacteria**, and **fungi** than others, which means that these places have greater biodiversity. For example, two thirds of the world's plant species are found in tropical rainforests.

It is a different story in the Arctic and Antarctica. There are fewer living things in **polar lands**, because it is hard to survive in these extreme conditions. In Antarctica, no **mammals** live on the land. No trees grow there, either, because it is the coldest and windiest place on Earth.

The Sonoran **Desert**, in the southwestern United States and Mexico, is an area of high biodiversity. Many plant species grow there.

Every animal on Earth can be sorted into a group, depending on its characteristics. There are six main groups of animal species:

ladybug

goldfish

Invertebrates: animals without backbones, such as insects, spiders, worms, and many more

Fish: scaly animals that live only in water, lay eggs, and breathe through gills

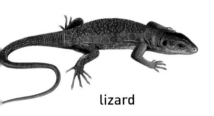

lizard

tree frog

Reptiles: animals with scaly skin that live on land or in water, such as lizards, crocodiles, turtles, and snakes

Amphibians: animals that live partly in water and partly on land, such as frogs, toads, and newts

sparrow

panda

Birds: animals that have wings, feathers, and beaks and lay eggs

Mammals: animals that have fur or hair and feed their young on milk made in the mother's body

Amazing places

The place where an animal lives is called a habitat.
Several species can share the same habitat—for
example, a pond may contain many different fish,
amphibians, insects, and plants. These living things
all depend on their particular habitat for food and
shelter. If their habitat is destroyed, animals can find
it difficult or impossible to survive. Habitats on land
include deserts, grasslands, and forests.

Rainforests provide a habitat
for thousands of different species.
These parrots are roosting on a fig
tree in the Amazon rainforest.

Oceans cover more than two thirds of Earth's surface and are home to more than a quarter of a million species of animals and plants. There are many different ocean habitats, such as **kelp forests** and **coral reefs**. Each ocean habitat shelters a different variety of species. In warm, tropical oceans, several kinds of fish, turtles, octopuses, and sea snakes live among coral reefs. These creatures are often brightly colored, so they are difficult to spot near the colorful coral.

These corals are near the north coast of West Papua, in Indonesia. More than 1,100 species of fish are found on the coral reef in this part of the world.

Underwater habitat
A coral reef looks like a colorful garden, but it does not contain any plants. Each type of coral is actually a colony of billions of tiny invertebrates, called polyps.

Living together

Animals and plants need food, water, and shelter. This means that they have to live in groups, sharing the same habitat and depending on each other to survive. A group of animals and plants that live together in a habitat like this is called an **ecosystem**. The environment is made up of many different ecosystems, some small and others much bigger.

Ecosystems can be huge—for example, an entire forest is an ecosystem. Birds, insects, mammals, and plants all shelter in a forest and rely on one another for food. But the same forest may also contain many smaller ecosystems. An oak tree can be an ecosystem all by itself, supporting a group of small creatures and plant species that share the same habitat and depend on each other.

This squirrel is eating an acorn—the animal and the nut both belong to the same ecosystem.

A lion hunts a zebra in the grasslands.

The grasslands of Africa have some amazing wildlife—and many different ecosystems. For example, lions, zebras, and grass are part of the same ecosystem. Packs of lions hunt herds of zebras, which feed on the grass. The lions, zebras, and grass all need to exist together in the ecosystem to keep it working.

An oak tree is an ecosystem for many plants and animals.

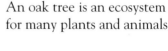

Branches and leaves: support insects such as bees and moths, birds such as sparrows and hawks, and climbing mammals such as squirrels

Trunk: supports insects

Roots and leaf litter: support bacteria, earthworms, fungi, and pill bugs

11

Earth's climates

The pattern of weather that you get in a place over a long period of time is called its climate. Climates vary around the world. However, different parts of the world have similar climates that provide habitats for similar plants and animals. These areas of similar climates are called biomes. Most biomes include several habitats. Some smaller biomes are unusual because they contain only one habitat. For example, arctic tundra is both a habitat and a biome.

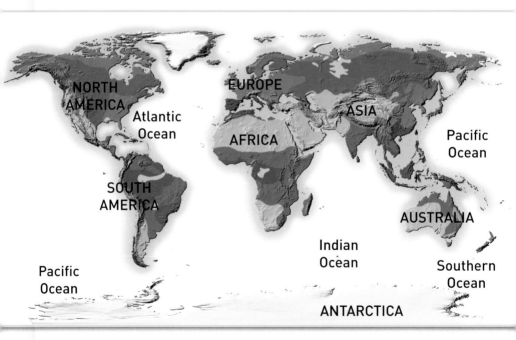

NORTH AMERICA

Atlantic Ocean

EUROPE

ASIA

AFRICA

Pacific Ocean

SOUTH AMERICA

AUSTRALIA

Pacific Ocean

Indian Ocean

Southern Ocean

ANTARCTICA

You can find the same type of biome on different parts of the planet.

In the Sonoran Desert, the large cardon cactus can store more than a ton of water in its stem to help it survive the hot, dry climate.

It is difficult for living things to survive in extreme climates, but animals and plants find ways of adapting to the conditions where they live. For example, in the Arctic, fox cubs stay warm in snowy dens. In deserts, cactus plants store water in their stems.

KEY
Polar
Arctic tundra
Mountains
Coniferous forests
Temperate forests
Tropical forests
Shrublands
Grasslands
Deserts
Wetlands
Coral reefs

In the winter, the arctic fox has an extra layer of fat and a thick fur coat to help it survive the icy cold.

Planet Earth

Earth is a planet in space. When we look at photos of our planet, we can see the oceans, the **continents**, and the swirling clouds in the **atmosphere**.

From space, Earth looks blue. That is because more than two thirds of it is covered with water.

The atmosphere is a layer of gases that protects Earth, absorbing harmful rays from the Sun and balancing the temperature. Gases in the atmosphere include nitrogen, **oxygen**, and **carbon dioxide**. There could be no life on Earth without the atmosphere.

All green plants take in **energy** from the Sun, water and **minerals** from the soil, and carbon dioxide from the air. They then give off water and oxygen into the atmosphere. If too many trees and green plants are cut down, levels of carbon dioxide will rise, disturbing the fine balance of Earth's atmosphere.

Green plants help balance the different gases in the atmosphere.

Weather and seasons

Weather forms in the lowest part of the atmosphere, up to 6 miles (10 kilometers) above the ground, within a layer of the atmosphere called the troposphere. Rain and snow form in clouds, and the movement of air in the atmosphere creates winds. The Sun's rays travel through the atmosphere to warm Earth and give us hot, sunny weather.

There are regular patterns of weather. Some parts of the world have four seasons. Summer is hot and sunny, fall is cool and windy, winter can be cold and snowy, and spring brings sunshine and showers.

Exosphere
6,000 mi.
(10,000 km)

Thermosphere
430 mi. (690 km)

Mesosphere
50 mi. (85 km)

Stratosphere
30 mi. (50 km)

Troposphere
0–9 mi.
(0–15 km)

There are five main layers in Earth's atmosphere.

In the summer, the Sun shines for longer and flowers bloom.

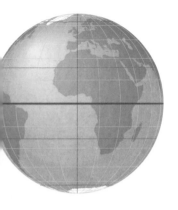

On a map, the equator is shown as a line around Earth. The areas around the equator are the hottest places on the planet.

The equator is an imaginary line that runs around the middle of Earth. In the parts of the world near the equator, it is very hot all year long. These parts are called the tropics. There are only two seasons in tropical places—we call them wet and dry seasons. The wet season is also known as the **monsoon** season.

In tropical countries, heavy monsoon rains can cause floods.

Earth's riches

Things from nature that are useful to people are called natural resources. Earth is rich in natural resources, such as metals and **fossil fuels**. These may be found under the ground or under the seabed. For example, aluminum and iron are metals that are found in mines underground.

The coal in this mine is hundreds of feet under the ground.

Gold is a precious metal that is sometimes used to make valuable coins.

Wood is a common material that is used to make practical things, like this bowl.

Fossil fuels are made from the decayed remains of dead plants and animals. They take hundreds of millions of years to form, deep under the ground. Oil, gas, and coal are different types of fossil fuels. Oil rigs drill under the surface of Earth to collect oil. Some oil rigs are on land, and others are out at sea.

We burn fossil fuels in order to provide energy for transportation, homes, and places of work. We are using them up so quickly that some scientists predict that coal may only last another few hundred years and that all our natural gas and oil may run out in less than 100 years.

Oil rigs drill for oil deep under the seabed.

Environment in danger

In some places, air pollution is so bad that people wear facemasks to try to avoid breathing in the pollution.

The environment faces many difficult problems and dangers. For example, we rely on natural resources, such as coal, oil, and gas, but we know that they will not last forever. We are overusing Earth's precious resources and upsetting the natural balance of the environment.

Pollution is harming many places on Earth. Pollution is any type of dirt or waste that damages the environment. Poisonous **chemicals** from factories and power plants are making the land, sea, and air less healthy and safe. Important habitats are being harmed, putting many rare species and fragile ecosystem in danger.

Some factories create smoke that contains harmful chemicals that pollute the air we breathe.

Scientists warn that temperatures around the world are rising faster than ever before. This is called **global warming**, and it is happening because humans are putting large amounts of harmful gases in Earth's atmosphere. These gases are trapping too much of the Sun's warmth in Earth's atmosphere. As a result, the world is slowly getting warmer.

The carbon cycle

Gases that help cause global warming are called greenhouse gases. One of the most important greenhouse gases is carbon dioxide. This gas is made when animals breathe and when any materials made from carbon are burned, such as fossil fuels.

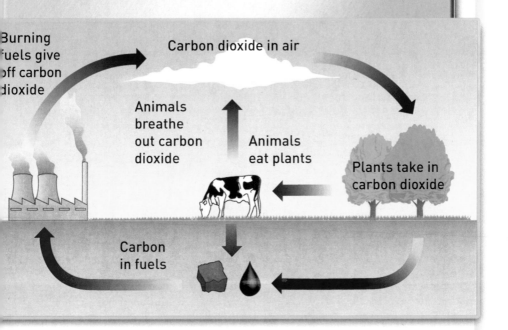

Burning fuels give off carbon dioxide

Carbon dioxide in air

Animals breathe out carbon dioxide

Animals eat plants

Plants take in carbon dioxide

Carbon in fuels

Disappearing habitats

Many habitats around the world are at risk. Every day, fragile habitats such as rainforests are destroyed to make way for cattle farms, mines, and other **industries**.

In the past 50 years, more than half of the world's rainforests have been destroyed.

The growing world population is a threat to animal habitats.

Some species of animals are put in danger because their habitats are disappearing. Rare animals may even die out completely because they can't adapt quickly enough to survive in new habitats.

There are currently more than seven billion people on the planet, and this number is getting bigger all the time. It is difficult to protect all animal habitats when so many humans need space to live and food to eat.

These corals in the Caribbean Sea have died as a result of global warming.

Pollution is a big problem for many habitats. For example, air pollution can mix with clouds, causing acid rain to fall. Over time, acid rain can kill trees and destroy large areas of forest.

Another danger for precious habitats is global warming. This is caused by humans putting high levels of harmful gases into the atmosphere. At a result, some coral reefs are dying because the oceans are getting warmer. Warmer water kills **algae** that live on the corals, and the corals do not have enough food to survive. Sadly, when the reefs die, so do all of the animals and plants that live on them.

Animals at risk

When the last member of a species dies out, we say that species has become **extinct**. Over the past hundred years, more species have become extinct than ever before. Some experts believe it will take only another hundred years for up to half of all the species on Earth to disappear.

Today, many animal species are in danger of becoming extinct. This is often because they are losing their natural habitat. For example, there are only about 30,000 orangutans left in the wild, and one third of all amphibian species are now **endangered**.

The last quagga
A quagga was a type of zebra that lived in southern Africa. It was hunted to extinction for its meat and leather. The last quagga died in a zoo in Amsterdam, in the Netherlands, in 1883.

Orangutans live in the rainforest. Their forest habitat is being cut down for timber and to make way for palm oil plantations.

Pollution is a threat to many animals. Garbage in the oceans is a hazard for endangered marine species, such as the leatherback turtle. Many turtles have died after swallowing plastic bags, balloons, or other floating plastic waste.

Turtles can mistake plastic bags for jellyfish and die after eating them.

Disasters caused by people

Disasters can happen when there are industrial accidents, such as when chemicals leak from a factory or when oil spills into the ocean. Animals are poisoned by this pollution and entire ecosystems are destroyed. Local communities and industries are also badly affected.

Long-term disaster

In 1986, there was an accident at a **nuclear power** plant at Chernobyl, in Ukraine, and 125,000 square miles (323,749 square kilometers) of land were **contaminated**. Many thousands of people died or became sick, and children born in the area have had serious health problems. The land around Chernobyl is still contaminated, and people and animals cannot live there safely.

These scientists are checking the levels of radiation on the land at Chernobyl, 20 years after the accident happened.

After the 2010 oil spill, there was a huge cleanup operation in the Gulf of Mexico. These boats pulled nets across the water to skim off some of the oil.

In May 2010, there was an explosion on an oil rig in the Gulf of Mexico. As a result, several million gallons of oil gushed into the sea. Many sea animals were killed in the Gulf, and coastal industries ground to a halt. People called it the worst environmental disaster in U.S. history.

Sea birds can drown if their feathers are soaked in oil. People have to clean off the oil for them.

Pollution problems

Worldwide, factories and transportation create huge amounts of pollution. Every minute of every day, many factories and farms leak **toxic** waste into the soil and into the water supply. Harmful gases are released into the air when materials are burned in power plants and factories.

Most of the plastic bags we use end up in landfill sites. They take hundreds of years to rot.

A lot of our garbage is taken to landfill sites, where it is crushed by bulldozers and buried in big holes in the ground. Poisonous chemicals may seep into the soil, and greenhouse gases such as methane may rise up into the atmosphere.

Sewage plants treat wastewater to remove harmful materials. But sometimes the waste can leak from these plants into nearby rivers. For example, in 2011, a big sewage spill in central China had terrible effects on the environment. In just three days, thousands of fish were killed in polluted rivers in Hubei Province.

This man is collecting dead fish from a polluted pond near the city of Wuhan, China.

Climate change

Different parts of the world have different climates. There is **evidence** that these climates are changing because of global warming. Scientists do not know exactly how much warmer Earth will get or how quickly this may happen. Many predict that temperatures will rise by 3.5°F (2°C) by 2050.

This may not sound like much, but if it happens, it will be very bad news for the environment. Some parts of the world may turn into desert, causing food and water shortages for millions of people. In India, much less rice and wheat could be produced. Global warming could change our weather patterns, including the amount of rain or snow that falls in different places. Storms may become more common in some parts of the world.

In the future, **famine** and **drought** could become even more common.

In the future, polar lands such as the Arctic and Antarctica may become warmer, and the rising temperatures could make the ice melt in these polar regions. This would make sea levels rise all over the world, flooding many coastal towns and cities. The results of this would be devastating.

The big melt
Polar ice is already melting faster than ever before because of global warming. This affects polar wildlife. For example, when arctic glaciers melt away, polar bears find it very difficult to survive.

This massive iceberg was formed when it broke away from an ice sheet in Antarctica.

Wild weather

In many parts of the world, there are extreme forms of weather. For example, in polar lands there are freezing blizzards, and in tropical countries there are huge storms called hurricanes, typhoons, or cyclones. Changing climate patterns are making the weather more extreme in some places. The huge storms in the tropics seem to be getting stronger and more dangerous.

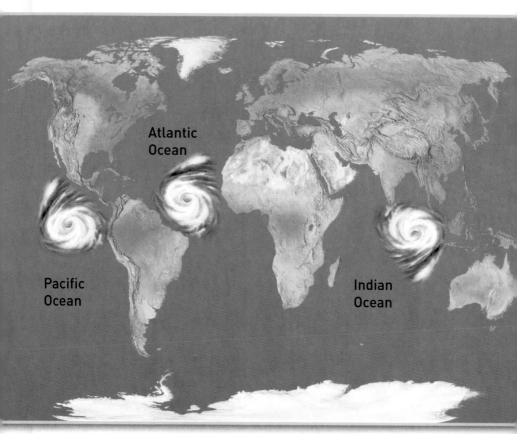

This map shows where the huge storms happen: cyclones in the Pacific Ocean, hurricanes in the Atlantic Ocean, and typhoons in Southeast Asia.

Are hurricanes getting worse?

In August 2005, Hurricane Katrina swept through New Orleans, Louisiana, causing serious floods. The hurricane destroyed about 275,000 homes, ten times more than any other **natural disaster** in U.S. history. Was Hurricane Katrina caused by climate change? There is no way to know for certain, but we do know that powerful hurricanes like this are likely to happen more often as a result of climate change.

Global warming makes droughts happen more often. If no rain falls or there is much less rain than usual, there is a drought. This means that there is not enough water and crops fail. People die because they do not have enough to drink or eat.

People cannot survive for very long without water. This boy in Cambodia collects water from a water pump in his village.

Conservation challenge

There are many things that people can do to reduce pollution, clean up the environment, and save endangered species. For example, we know that when habitats are destroyed, animals are put at risk. We can try to stop this from happening. This type of work is called conservation.

Conservation projects can turn fragile habitats into national parks and wildlife reserves. In these protected zones, the land is closely cared for, hunting is banned, and the animals are kept safe.

This rare mountain gorilla lives in a national park in Uganda, in Africa.

Rainforests have been growing for more than 400 million years. They are called the "lungs" of the planet because they take in carbon dioxide from the atmosphere and give off oxygen. Many people are fighting to protect the rainforests.

These conservation workers are putting an electronic tag on a harpy eagle in the Amazon rainforest.

Understanding conservation

People need to learn about the environment in order to understand why it must be protected. National parks and wildlife reserves run education programs to teach children and adults about conservation. The money that tourists pay to visit these places is used to help take care of endangered species and habitats.

35

Animal rescue

Conservation groups are working hard to save
endangered animals. For example, many charities
have set up projects to protect animals that are in
danger of becoming extinct. You can support this
work by donating money—for example, you can pay
to "adopt" a rare animal, such as a polar bear or tiger.

This map shows where some important conservation
work is taking place around the world.

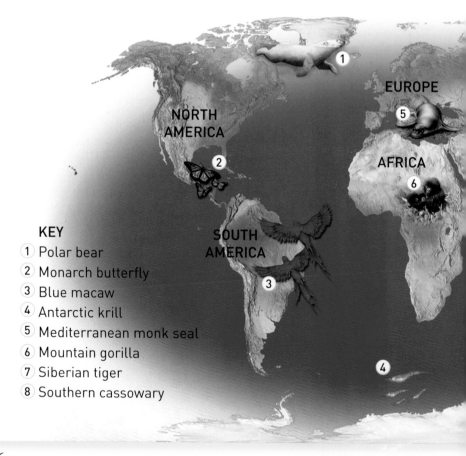

KEY
1. Polar bear
2. Monarch butterfly
3. Blue macaw
4. Antarctic krill
5. Mediterranean monk seal
6. Mountain gorilla
7. Siberian tiger
8. Southern cassowary

When an animal is endangered, it means that there are not many of its kind left. Endangered animals are encouraged to have babies, or breed, so that the population of that species can begin to grow.

Sometimes breeding programs are very successful. In the Amazon rainforest, a monkey called the golden lion tamarin was almost extinct. In the 1970s, there were fewer than 200 golden lion tamarins in the wild. A conservation program prevented this animal from dying out. Now, there are more than 1,000 in the wild, and their numbers are rising.

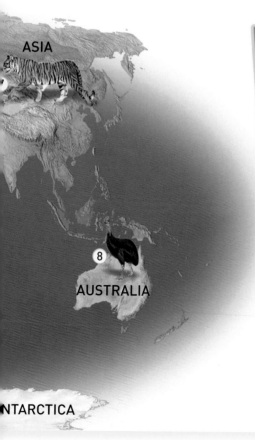

ASIA

8

AUSTRALIA

NTARCTICA

A lot of the golden lion tamarin's forest habitat has been destroyed, but these monkeys have been saved from extinction because of work by conservation groups.

"Clean" power

Some ways of producing energy make far less pollution than fossil fuels do. For example, solar power turns the Sun's rays into electricity. It is clean to produce, and the Sun's rays will not run out. A huge solar power plant has been built in Spain, for example. It produces electricity for 180,000 homes in the city of Seville.

Solar panels on rooftops can provide power for our homes.

Wind turns the long blades of wind turbines, producing large amounts of electricity for towns and cities. Out at sea, wave power can also be used to make electricity.

In a wind farm, many turbines work together to generate electricity.

The Three Gorges Dam in China is the world's largest electricity plant.

The power of flowing water can also be used to make electricity. This is called hydroelectric power. Dams are built across rivers to create hydroelectric power. The biggest dam in the world is the Three Gorges Dam in China. It generates as much electricity as 18 coal-fired power plants without causing air pollution. In spite of this, many people are unhappy about the Three Gorges Dam. Cities, towns, and villages were flooded to make way for it, and more than one million people were forced to move out of their homes.

Saving energy

We can help the environment by saving energy. If we use less electricity and fuel, we will not have to produce as much of it in the first place. There are many things we can do to save energy. For example, in the winter we can wear warmer clothes inside instead of turning up the heat. We can also try to stop heat from escaping from our homes. Remember to close the doors and windows!

Flip the switch
Always turn off the light when you leave a room. Don't leave your TV, computer, or other electrical gadgets on standby, because this uses almost as much energy as when they are fully on.

Riding a bike is good
for the environment
and keeps you healthy
and fit too.

There are more than 600 million cars in the world,
and many of them make unnecessary journeys. Think
of different ways of traveling, such as walking, cycling,
carpooling, or using public transportation. Buses and
trains carry a lot of people, so they don't use up as much
gas or other fuel per person as cars do.

Waste watch

We don't just waste energy—we also waste huge amounts of food. Every year, about 39 million tons (35 million metric tons) of food is thrown away in the United States. Much of this food is not even touched or opened before it ends up in the garbage can. We can easily cut back on how much food we waste if we buy only what we really need.

Food waste
Grocery stores and supermarkets sell food in large containers. This leads to waste, as we cannot always eat all of the food we buy before it expires. Write a shopping list to stop you from buying things you don't need and don't have room to store.

Volunteers show that they can make a good meal using rejected food. Supermarkets throw away huge amounts of fruit and vegetables because they do not look perfect.

In some parts of the world, there is not enough water for everyone. In places where there is more water, it is often wasted. As climate change affects the amount of rain that falls around the world, we will need to be much more careful about water in the future.

Turn it off!
Turn off the faucet when you brush your teeth. This saves a lot of water every day.

Reuse and recycle

Making things in factories uses up energy and natural resources and creates pollution. The more we throw away, the more new goods have to be made to replace them. It is much better for the environment if we reuse things instead. This means fewer new things need to be made, and there is not as much waste and pollution.

If you can't reuse something yourself, give it away or sell it so that someone else can reuse it.

You can get a bargain at a secondhand sale and help protect the environment at the same time.

When something old and unwanted is **recycled**, it is made into something new and useful. Recycling is good for the environment because it saves the energy and natural resources that are needed to make new materials.

This fleece was made from about 20 recycled plastic bottles.

Be extra careful with your garbage. Before you throw it away, sort it out to be recycled. Always put glass, paper, cardboard, steel, aluminum, and plastic bottles in recycling containers. Don't mix them up with materials that can't be recycled, such as hard plastic and Styrofoam.

Remember—our environment is amazing. We must all do our part to keep it that way!

Do recycle:
- glass and plastic bottles
- paper and cardboard
- steel and aluminum cans

45

Glossary

adapt to change in order to survive in new conditions

algae very tiny, plantlike things that live in water

atmosphere the layer of gases around Earth

bacteria very tiny living things

carbon dioxide one of the greenhouse gases in the atmosphere that cause global warming

chemical another word for a substance

contaminated containing harmful, unhealthy substances

continent one of the seven large landmasses in the world

coral reef an underwater structure made from tiny sea animals, called polyps

desert an area of very dry land

drought a long period without rain

ecosystem a group of living things that share a habitat and depend on one another

endangered in danger of dying out

energy the power to do things or to make things work

evidence proof of something

extinct when an animal or plant species dies out completely

famine a terrible shortage of food

fossil fuel a source of energy that is buried deep under the ground, such as gas, oil, or coal

fungi (singular: fungus) a group of living things, including mushrooms and toadstools, that are not plants or animals

global warming the rise in the overall temperature of Earth's atmosphere

industry a business that makes and sells things

kelp forest an area in the ocean where a lot of kelp (a type of seaweed) grows

mammal an animal with fur or hair that drinks its mother's milk when it is young

mineral a natural material that is part of rocks and soil

monsoon a wind that brings heavy rain and floods to India and Southeast Asia

natural disaster a natural event that brings great destruction— for example, a volcanic eruption, earthquake, tsunami, storm, flood, or wildfire

nuclear power energy that is produced from a controlled nuclear reaction in a power plant

oxygen one of the gases in the air. We breathe it to stay alive

polar lands the areas around the North and South poles

pollution harmful chemicals that make a place or thing dirty or poison it

recycle to convert waste materials into new materials

species a group of plants or animals of the same kind, which breed together to produce young

toxic poisonous

tropical from a hot, wet part of the world near the equator

Index

If you have enjoyed reading
this book, look out for more in
the Kingfisher Readers series!

Collect
and read
them all!

KINGFISHER READERS: LEVEL 4

The Arctic and Antarctica ☐
Flight ☐
Human Body ☐
Pirates ☐
Rivers ☐
Sharks ☐
Spiders—Deadly Predators ☐
Weather ☐

KINGFISHER READERS: LEVEL 5

Ancient Egyptians ☐
The Changing Environment ☐
Explorers ☐
Hurricanes ☐
Rainforests ☐
Record Breakers—The Fastest ☐
Record Breakers—The Most Dangerous ☐
Space ☐

For a full list of Kingfisher Readers books, plus
guidance for teachers and parents and activities
and fun stuff for kids, go to the Kingfisher Readers
website: **www.kingfisherreaders.com**